classic soul for piano

CW00448231

Wise Publications
part of The Music Sales Group

London/New York/Paris/Sydney/Copenhagen/Berlin/Madrid/Tokyo

Band Of Gold

Words & Music by Ronald Dunbar & Edith Wayne

Everyday People

Words & Music by Sylvester Stewart

so on and so on and scoo-by doo bee doo, (M) oh,_____ sha_

____ sha, we got to live__ to-geth - er._____

(F) There is a yel-low one that won't ac-cept the black one, that

won't ac-cept the red one, that won't ac-cept the white one. Dif-f'rent strokes__ for

8

(M) *Verse 2:*

    I am no better and neither are you
    We are the same whatever we do
    You love me, you hate me, you know me and then
    You can't figure out the bag I'm in
    I am everyday people.

(F)   There is a long hair that doesn't like the short hair
    For being such a rich one that will not help the poor one
    Different strokes for different folks
    And so on, and so on
    And scooby doo be doo.

(M) Oh sha sha, we got to live together.

For Your Precious Love

Words & Music by Arthur Brooks, Richard Brooks & Jerry Butler

Spoken: 1. Into each life a little rain must fall. And you
(Verses 2 & 3 see block lyrics)

know every day cannot be Sunday, every smile is not a smile of happiness. And every tear that is shedded is not a tear of joy.

I'd like to dedicate this song to all of you lovers out there because maybe you have a loved one that's far, far away.

love _____ can't ev-er be. _____ 5. I've learned to en - dure _____

Spoken: 6. You know something ladies and especially you ladies
(Verse 7 see block lyric) I'd like to speak to,

because you know something ladies, if you gotta man,
I don't care what kind of a

man you got, he wants you to get down on your knees
every once in a while and kinda crawl

to him. But you know, I got a man somewhere out
there I don't mind

crawling to. Sometimes I wake up in the midnight hours,
tears rolling down my

face and when I look around for my man and I
can't find him, hey, I fall a little

12

lower, look a little higher, kinda pray
to the lord. Because I

always believe that the Lord can help you
if nobody else could. 7. But sometimes

8. Darl - - - - - - - - - ing,— darl - ing
(Verse 9 see block lyric)

don't you know— that I love you too much?— Yeah,— yeah.— Oh,—

Fall down on my knees— and prayed my ba - by please— oh, can you

tell my man that I love him. Yes I will.___ Oh._____

Verse 2: (Spoken)
You know, I can imagine when you're all alone in the wee wee hours of the night
Why don't you get yourself a piece of paper and a pencil and sit down
And, Lord have mercy, decide to write
Knowing all the time that this letter that you write may not be a comfort to your loved one
But let me tell you something you can say
You can say "Darling, for your precious love, I give you the world on a silver plate"
Huh, but you know as well as I that you'd be telling a great big lie
And you don't wanna do that to your loved one
Neither would I.

Verse 3: (Spoken)
But you can say "Darling, for your precious love I'd climb the highest mountain"
You know something ladies and gentlemen
You could even go out as far a telling him or her that you'd try to swim the deepest sea
But I think if you always sit back, relax, put your mind at rest and listen to me
I think I can give you a better understanding of what I'm trying to say, mm.

Verse 5:
I've learned to endure, oh and I
…wanted you…
Lady…
I was so lonely… and so blue
Good God am I, messed when I found you.

Verse 7:
But sometimes I think He don't even hear me
So I have to fall a little lower on my knees, look a little higher
Kinda raise my voice a little higher
And this is what sing when I call for my man
I expressly want you ladies to listen to me because maybe you can try this
It might help you every once in a while
This is what you sing when you call on your man
Learn to endure.

Verse 9:
With your friends and mine
There's nothing in this whole wide world I wouldn't do for you darling
No, and I won't go
Lord I gotta see my baby again
I gotta tell my man that I love him
One more time.

Go Now

Words & Music by Larry Banks & Milton Bennett

just what you in-tend to do now._____ Cos

how ma-ny times have to tell you, darl-in', darl-in', darl-in', darl-in', darl-

-in', I'm still in love, still in love— with

1.
you now. 2. We've al-rea-dy said_____

Verse 2:
We've already said, so long
I don't want to see you go
But boy you had better
Go now, go now
Go now, go now
Don't you even try

Bridge 2:
To tell me that you really don't
Want to see it in this way now.
Don't you know
If you really meant what you said
Darlin', darlin', darlin'
I wouldn't have to keep on begging you
Begging you, begging you
Begging you to stay.

Go now *etc.*

Green Onions

Music by Booker T. Jones, Steve Cropper, Al Jackson Jr & Lewie Steinberg

21

I Get The Sweetest Feeling

Words & Music by Van McCoy & Alicia Evelyn

22

you._____ When you turn on___ your smile___

I feel my heart___ go wild.___ I'm___ like a child

_____ with a brand new toy.___ And I get the

sweet-est feel - ing, hon-ey the sweet-est. (Sweet-est feel-

Verse 2:

The warmer your kiss, the deeper you touch me baby
The deeper your touch, the more you thrill me
It's more than I can stand girl
When you hold my hand
I feel so grand that I could cry.

And I get the (sweetest feeling)
Mama the sweetest (sweetest feeling)
Baby the sweetest (sweetest feeling)
Loving you.

Verse 3:

The greater your love, the stronger you hold me baby
The stronger your hold, the more I need you
With every passing day
I love you more in every way
I'm in love to stay and I wanna say.

I get the (sweetest feeling)
Baby the sweetest (sweetest feeling)
Honey the sweetest (sweetest feeling)
Loving you.

I Got You (I Feel Good)

Words & Music by James Brown

Verse 2, 3 & 4:
I feel nice, like sugar and spice
I feel nice, like sugar and spice
So nice, so nice since I got you.

Verse 5:
I feel good, like I knew that I would now
I feel good, I knew that I would
So good, so good since I got you.

I Say A Little Prayer

Words by Hal David
Music by Burt Bacharach

While comb - ing my hair now and wond-'ring what dress to wear now

I say a lit - tle prayer for you. For - ev - er, for - ev - er, you'll

stay in my heart and I will love you for - ev - er and ev - er. We

nev-er will part. Oh, how I love you, To - ge-ther, to - ge-ther, that's how it must be. To

30

Verse 2:
I run for the bus, dear
While riding I think of us, dear.
I say a little prayer for you.
At work I just take time
And all through my coffee break time
I say a little prayer for you.

I'd Rather Go Blind

Words & Music by Ellington Jordan & Billy Foster

1. Some-thing told me it was ov - - er, (Yeah)
(Verse 2 see block lyric)

when I saw— you— and her— talk-ing.

Some-thing deep down in my soul— said "cry— girl," (cry,

cry,——)when I saw— you and that girl— walk-ing— down.— Ooh,——

—— I would rath-er, I would rath-er go— blind—— boy,

34

Verse 2:
I was just sitting here thinking
Of your kiss and your warm embrace
When the reflection in the glass
That I held to my lips now babe
Revealed the tears that was on my face.

I would rather be blind *etc.*

In The Midnight Hour

Words & Music by Steve Cropper & Wilson Pickett

Let's Stay Together

Words & Music by Al Green, Willie Mitchell & Al Jackson

41

Verse 2:
And they're sayin' things, babe
Since we've been together
Ooh, loving you forever
Is what I need
Let me be the one you come running to
I'll never be untrue.

Verse 3:
Why, why people break up,
Oh, turn around and make up
I just can't to see
You'd never do that to me
Just being around you is all I see.

Midnight Train To Georgia

Words & Music by Jim Weatherly

leav - in'___ (leav-in') on___ that mid - night train_to Geor - gia.(Leavin' on that mid - night train. _)

Yes, said he's go - in' back (go-in' back_ to find) to a sim-pler

place and time. Oh yes he is. And I'll___ be with him (I know you will_
(When-ev-er he takes that ride_ guess who's gonna be right by_ his side._)

___) on___ that mid - night train to Geor - gia. Hey.___
(Leav-in on the mid - night train_ to Geor-gia, woo woo!)

Verse 2:
He kept dreamin' that someday he'd be the star
(A superstar, but he didn't get far)
But he sure found out the hard way
That dreams don't always come true
So he turned all his hopes
And he even sold his old car
Bought a one-way ticket back to the life he once knew.

He's leavin' *etc.*

46

Private Number

Words & Music by William Bell & Booker T. Jones

Verse 2: (Girl)
I'm sorry you couldn't call me when you got home
But other fellas kept on calling when you were gone.
So I had the number changed but I'm not acting strange.
Welcome home, nothing's wrong.

Baby baby baby etc.

Rescue Me

Words & Music by Carl Smith & Raynard Miner

53

take my hand,— come on ba-by and be my man,— cos I love— you, cos I want— you, can't you see that I'm lone-ly.— Mm,— mm.— Take me ba-by, love me ba-by, need me ba-by.— Mm,—

55

Verse 2:
Rescue me
Come on and take my heart
Take your love
And comfort every part.

Cos I'm lonely *etc.*

Son Of A Preacher Man

Words & Music by John Hurley & Ronnie Wilkins

58

was he was, mm,——— yes he was.——

1.

2.

How well I—— re-mem - ber

the look that was in—— his eyes,——   steal-ing kiss - es from me—— on the sly,—

59

Verse 2:
Being good isn't always easy
No matter how hard I try.
When he started sweet talking to me,
He'd come and tell me everything is all right,
He'd kiss and tell me everything is all right,
Can't get away again tonight.

Stay With Me Baby

Words & Music by George David Weiss & Jerry Ragovoy

Verse 2:
Who did you touch,
When you needed tenderness.
I gave you so much,
And in return I found happiness.
Baby what did I do,
Maybe I was too good,
Just too good for you.
No no, I can't believe,
You'd really leave.

Stay with me *etc.*

(Take A Little) Piece Of My Heart

Words & Music by Jerry Ragovoy & Bert Berns

Verse 2:
You're out on the street (looking good)
And you know deep down in your heart that ain't right
And oh, you never hear me when I cry at night
I tell myself that I can't stand the pain
But when you hold me in your arms I say it again.

So come on *etc.*

Try A Little Tenderness

Words & Music by Harry Woods, Jimmy Campbell & Reg Connelly

gen - tle, makes it ea - si - er to bear.

You won't re - gret it, wo - men don't for - get it, love is their whole hap - pi -

- ness. It's all so ea - sy, try a lit - tle ten - der -

- ness.

- ness.

Published by
Wise Publications,
8/9 Frith Street, London, W1D 3JB, England.

Exclusive distributors:
Music Sales Limited,
Distribution Centre, Newmarket Road, Bury St Edmunds,
Suffolk, IP33 3YB, England.

Music Sales Pty Limited,
120 Rothschild Avenue, Rosebery,
NSW 2018, Australia.

Order No. AM91477
ISBN 0-7119-3714-1
This book © Copyright 2004 by Wise Publications.

Complier Nick Crispin.

Printed in Malta by Interprint Limited.

www.musicsales.com

Your Guarantee of Quality:

As publishers, we strive to produce every book to the
highest commercial standards.

Particular care has been given to specifying acid-free, neutral-sized paper
made from pulps which have not been elemental chlorine bleached.

This pulp is from farmed sustainable forests and was produced
with special regard for the environment.

Throughout, the printing and binding have been planned to ensure
a sturdy, attractive publication which should give years of enjoyment.

If your copy fails to meet our high standards, please inform us
and we will gladly replace it.